SO-DTB-091

THDRAWN

Simone Swan: Adobe Building

Dennis Dollens

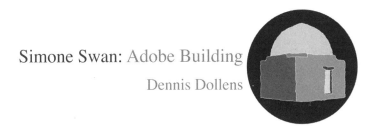

WITHDRAWN

3 1336 07406 8157

SITES Books • New Mexico

For my brother Allen

Lumen, Inc.
SITES Books
40 Camino Cielo
Santa Fe, New Mexico
87506
lumenbooks.org

Lumen, Inc. is a non-profit,
tax-exempt organization.
SITES Books is an imprint
of Lumen, Inc.

©2005 Dennis L. Dollens
tumbletruss.com
exodesic@mac.com
ISBN: 0-930829-58-1
ISBN: 9780930829582
Printed in the USA

Distribution
Consortium Book Sales
800 283-3572
www.cbsd.com

Adobe Alliance Logo
and all photographs unless
credited otherwise:
Dennis Dollens

A traditional earth plaster of mud, sand, straw, manure tea,
prickly pear juice, and water after mixing at Simone Swan's
Earth Plaster Workshop. This mixture is only one of the possible
plasters suitable for biomimetic study.

Introduction: Biomimetic Adobe

A little while ago we thought of the atoms as we thought of bricks, as solid building materials, as substantial matter, as unit masses of lifeless stuff, and behold! These bricks are boxes, treasure boxes, boxes full of the intensest force.
H. G. Wells. *The World Set Free.*

A little while ago most of us thought of adobe as a solid building material of an inert, impoverished nature. Yet, these walls and bricks, these boxes of dried earth are full of the *intensest* forces and chemical reactions. We can now see that what we once thought of as dumb is starting to emerge, in light of new material sciences and biomimetics, as smart; as elements that nature provides with what science considers advanced properties known as phase changes. Adobe, reconsidered as advanced and alive, and adobe respected in terms of traditional building, is part of the path I want to travel in these pages.

When Gottfried Semper theorized the birth of architecture in craft and technology—through weaving, pottery, and knotting, for example—he gave a perspective to architecture in which building is the process of assuming craft knowledge and cultural accumulation. A kind of physical, material ontology in which mud and plant fiber, wood and stone, come to be seen as imbued with meta-qualities and as distinct from the natural environment where they originated yet, at the same time, retaining in their physical being the components and

For an introduction to biomimetics see:

Benyus, Janine M. *Innovation Inspired by Nature: Biomimicry.* New York, NY, Quill. 1997.

Ball, Philip. *Made to Measure: New Materials for the 21st Century.* Princeton, NJ, Princeton University Press. 1999.

Dollens, Dennis. *DBA: Digital-Botanic Architecture.* Santa Fe, NM, SITES Books. 2005.

links to their original nature. (Not surprisingly, structures made from such materials signal deep-rooted natural connections between viewers and users). While the weaving of plant fiber into mats and the making of mud-and-stone architecture represent an ongoing, worldwide building tradition, in much of the developing world, these craft technologies have, for the most part, been eagerly abandoned when and where Western industrial development has become invasive. Nevertheless, today, in an age of appreciating biological understanding, it is important to re-evaluate traditional, natural materials with curiosity and deference as well as with biomimetic receptivity. I'll come back to biomimetics later but, for now, let me say that I see a process of visual and scientific biomimetics as a two-way path that can lead to both traditional building communities and, equally, impact new architectural, even avant-garde, development, using mud—adobe.

But first, keep in mind that adobe is not a singular codified substance made according to one formula: once mud is variously mixed with differing elements, molded, and hardened, it becomes a technical product of enormous sophistication, one that coevolved with trial-and-error techniques over eons of human development and did so in many different cultures. So, not only is adobe regional in its application to differing geographic building styles, it is also regional in terms of its chemical composition—muds of various mineral qualities mixed with diverse elements, from lime to cement to horse dung to paper to straw, etc., sun-baked or dried, all compose the class adobe, which is comprised of specifically different bricks with different levels of efficiency, both structural and thermal. Extrapolating from the archaic time frame of community experimentation with adobe building and mud plastering and their varied palette of material ingredients, we can begin to understand that culture and technology exert evolutionary forces on what is essentially a hardened patch of earth, harvested and stacked, to make shelters.

In our own time, we may further extrapolate from one contemporary organization, the Bioneers—beginning its weekly environmental broadcast with the words: "It's all alive, it's all connected"—the idea that there is still much left to be learned and evolved from and with mud. We may recall that mud, a compound of organic and inorganic elements—the home of various microorganisms—is alive—as Goethe said: "Und jades stäuben lebt" (And every particle of dust lives.) This fact is significantly demonstrated by medical traditions that use mud to heal and seal open wounds—a procedure in which mud's micro-organisms come into contact with human or animal micro-organisms to heal and prevent infection. Further use of mud, say as body-plasters, figures as a cosmetic application, while mud baths are soothing, cleansing, and meditative events. Mud wrestling is entertaining (to some). We are still culturally and physically connected with mud, beyond farming and gardening (and off-road landscape destruction) in many ways not generally at the tip of our consciousness and not generally considered as related to architecture.

To think about adobe in the developed

Workshops hosted by Adobe Alliance and directed by Simone Swan are annual events at the Swan House in Presidio, Texas.
www.adobealliance.org

world in this era of advanced composite materials (often poisonous), advanced construction techniques (mostly shoddy), and advanced environmental danger (mostly unregulated by the government) requires some re-evaluation of materials and material values within today's social, economic, political, and aesthetic context. The December 4, 2004 issue of *The Economist* carried a special technological report with an article called "The Rise of the Green Building," which began with an account of horrifying statistics: "In America, buildings account for 65% of total energy use and 30% of greenhouse-gas emissions." Obviously, architecture is moving in the wrong direction—except for a few green practices and practitioners. Equally obvious, adobe is not a panacea, not a large-scale answer. But examining mudworks and some construction examples employing adobe may elicit a model for extending principles and properties of adobe to other materials and processes while also supporting the use and knowledge of traditional adobeworks and workings.

For example, since biomimetics is a scientific process for viewing natural objects and organisms—to study their organic systems, chemical reactions, and growth cycles in order to appropriate specific qualities, such as hardness, softness, reflectivity, conductivity, secretion mechanisms, bonding properties, etc., as well as for new uses in industrial, medical, and environmental substances—then looking biomimetically to mud and its adobe relatives is a starting point for considering what other properties, found in other organisms or organic systems, might be considered for a next step in the evolution of mud building.

Adobe is a material assembled and manufactured through a technology as old as civilization and one related secondarily, and a bit irrelevantly, in my context, to baking—a globally discovered mud recipe that could not be explained scientifically for thousands of years. It is a material produced with primary ingredients involving basic chemical bonds and changes, achieved through molecular bonds and heat. Still, the material survived and evolved. The chemical process in adobe, like that in bread or cake (in adobe, ingredients such as decomposed organic matter, straw, silica, salts, and water; in bread, plant matter, water, salt, leavening) offers an interesting story and one ripe for telling as well as for resultant biological and biomimetic experimentation because of the potential for new ingredients and/or biological reactions (within the mud) and thus for an enhanced adobe performance, even while adhering to a traditional organic recipe for the mud bricks. Basically, however, mud building, like bread making, became for early civilizations a primary and integrated social activity. Today, a new biological investigation could point out and preserve relationships and continuums between traditional materials and building and compatible new biomimetic formulas, leading to green-construction possibilities and greener adobe—becoming a subset of traditional adobe; I'm not suggesting it as a replacement.

Adobe, as we know it, may have future life as a biologically evolved, contemporary material, even while maintaining its historical materiality and building properties. A more intelligent adobe is desirable. Perhaps new discoveries in organic chemistry will add to the list of adobe compounds, ingredients that sustain 100% of adobe's organic qualities at the same time that new chemical reactions stimulate improved abilities and properties, such as repelling water or increasing tensile strength (adobe is strong only under compression) or reducing its weight without losing its compression strength. I'm not suggesting a crude process like dumping cement into adobe or adding petrochemical plastics; but I am suggesting that the hardness of some seashells, for example, might provide clues for revolutionizing adobe's strength and durability. (Remember that the material of seashells is organic and secreted in liquid form, not theoretically incompatible with the liquid mud stage of adobe production). A biomimetic investigation of this type posits a potential brick that materially and culturally evolves in the same manner that adobe has always evolved. At the same time, an evolved biomimetic adobe product would allow a wider spectrum of users a way into adobe construction, permitting the spraying of adobe, for example, without losing the qualities of an earth structure while still gaining the ability to create greater curvature and organic shapes.

The technology and the continuing potential for developing mud materials as elements of construction is only part of my focus here. I began with that focus in order to establish a view of adobe as neither relegated to the ghetto of rich-house building nor marginalized as a niche material. Further, I wanted to acknowledge that in this era of genetic engineering and genetically modified organisms, a watchdog approach to appropriate biological sciences, not a knee-jerk rejection, might serve mudworks evolution more intelligently. If we establish links to new and traditional thinking about adobe as well as building, and, the evolution of materials in general, we could focus a discussion on advanced green materials for more responsible building.

I have often daydreamed of a light, thin adobe — like a skin and related to those mud crusts you find on dried riverbeds. A strong mud skin that might be secreted or sprayed onto a building frame; a skin containing microphotovoltaics, with the potential for opening pores for ventilation; a skin that sequesters air-borne carbon and functions like an environmental filter and sensor; a skin that someday might include bio-illumination; a skin, then, with qualities of a plant's leaf and a jellyfish's biological lighting system. Yet such biomimetic exploration is for another book. For a dream different.

Such biomimetic experimentation is not ultimately incompatible with the next section of this essay, because this dream material illustrates that I am thinking of adobe radically, as a material for new construction but equally appropriate for traditional building. An adobe future consistent with traditional mud building, one involving a cultural and intellectual exchange with science and technology, is possible although traditional builders as well as scientists seem to avoid looking to that future.

Finally, I note these views because they have been stimulated by my friendship with Simone Swan and are grounded in a line of thought influenced by her concentration on adobe, even though she focuses in a different direction, she has told me she finds some of the above interesting and would support deeper investigations into materials. But, because of limited help and resources such research is not her immediate focus; her focus is to build and to teach; and since it is building and teaching that opened this adobe dialogue, it is to that work that I now turn.

Simone Swan: Adobe Building

I started thinking about adobe because of living in Santa Fe, New Mexico for the last ten years. Seeded before that by having visited New Mexico to see pueblo architecture and the adobe-domed and vaulted mosque in Abiquiu designed by Hassan Fathy, my thoughts took root only after seeing the buildings designed by Simone Swan and discussing adobe and her interest in bringing Fathy's construction forms and some of his design philosophy to the American Southwest.

Simone Swan.

I am now addressing a few buildings by Simone Swan and Adobe Alliance that, in addition to being beautiful and environmentally sound, illustrate such a cultural transference of important ideas and structural/architectural forms across geography, time, and tradition—from Egypt (ancient and modern) to Texas and New Mexico. (This transference is different from, but ideologically related to, the cultural/material evolution of adobe discussed in the introduction.) The transfer also involves evaluation of materials and considerations of different adobe qualities for building in climates and cultures as varied as those of Egypt and the Southwestern U.S. Swan's transfer of appropriate segments of Fathy's design philosophy and forms from her time in his Cairo studio demonstrates that the importation of such beautiful structures—Nubian vault and dome, for example—offers important structural, environmental, and cultural contributions to mud building in the U.S. In this sense, her application of foreign, observed qualities and forms across

Photo: Yasmina Rossi

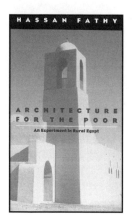

Hassan Fathy. *Architecture for the Poor: An Experiment in Rural Egypt.* Chicago, IL, University of Chicago Press. 1973.

time and space to a locally existing building typology (Southwest adobe tradition) is one kind of biomimetic appropriation and reapplication. Swan had seen a functional and useful form in a foreign setting and has studied, discovered, and invented ways of hybridizing that form with an appropriate and sympathetic host: adobe architecture in the deserts of the United States and Mexico.

Swan's buildings are little architectural revolutions in adobe and mud plasters. Her work embodies poetic aesthetic forms in earth bricks, manifested in plan and elevation. Even as her buildings highlight ideas and examples of form and technical transference between cultures, Swan is not imposing Egyptian forms on Southwestern building sites or clients. No, she is hybridizing and, when appropriate, incorporating Egyptian vaults and domes that tectonically take root beautifully.

While these well-rooted structures are rigorously traditional in their building techniques and primary construction materials, they do not scoff, nor does Swan, at environmentally compatible technical and mechanical systems for pumping water, heating, and generating electricity. Swan's work is an environmental as well as an architectural hybrid, and moreover her technical/artistic transference embodies and demonstrates her commitment to political and environmental action, including ideas emerging from the practice of permaculture site analysis.

From viewing photographs of Swan's buildings you can intuit her as an environmentally sensitive designer. But photographs, for the most part, don't reveal solar orientation, attention to prevailing winds, the creation of shade for garden and patio, and, where possible, the use of photovoltaic and windmill power. Neither do photographs hint at her basic techniques, or the possibilities for others to build in the manner of the Swan House, constructed at a smaller scale for middle- and low-income families; or that Swan has and continues to present her building as one alternative to affordable housing in the Big Bend region between Mexico and Texas. Yet, it is also clear that she will build in any dry and arid environment she is invited into.

A further political commitment is Swan's dedication to encouraging and teaching women to enter into construction employment—this most fully exemplified in her teaching and employing María Jesús (Jesusita) Jiménez, who has become Swan's primary construction manager as well as a co-spokesperson for adobe building and the Adobe Alliance in addition to developing her own independent building career.

You would predict from Swan's career as a foundation executive in New York and Houston that her arrival into building was wide of the mark. Her decision, first, to study with Hassan Fathy and, then, to build with and teach his ideas to communities along the US/Mexico border is complex, leading her along a difficult and solitary path. Yet her few buildings must be taken into view along with her larger intentions of teaching and of founding the non-profit educational organization, Adobe Alliance. Her goal of environmental action and educational redress through physical building falls under the rubric she applies in Adobe Alliance's motto: Adobe is Political.

Over the last five years I have known and talked with Swan during summers when she resides in Santa Fe. In 2002 I first visited her at the house she built in Presidio and where she has based Adobe Alliance. But it was only in July of 2003 that I began to question her with the idea of writing this essay. Swan is a gifted cook and we met many times over her Thai curries and talked. Often general but equally often focused, our conversations illuminated some points important to cover here. I was curious how someone coming from Swan's background of directing a cultural foundation, someone based in New York and then Houston, decided to go to Cairo and study with the master Egyptian architect, Hassan Fathy, and then, further, how she decided to transfer that learning to the geographically and culturally isolated Big Bend area of West Texas.

Swan's elegant and urbane conversation not only weaves her own story, it also entwines parallel cultural and social history, embracing the listener, welcoming questions, asides, and diversions. For this essay I'll bypass most biographical information (she is working on her own book) but some basic chronology is useful. Here is how Swan described meeting Fathy in an article she wrote for *Aramco World.*

> It was during a dinner party in 1972 that I heard my host announce the completion of a film on "the greatest architect of the century, Hassan Fathy" . . . All I could think was "Hassan who?" Yet I

was the director of the philanthropic Menil Foundation in Houston, which was active in art and architecture, and I considered myself well-acquainted with the leaders of contemporary architecture. . . . The next day I read Fathy's seminal book *Construire avec le peuple* [published in English as *Architecture for the Poor*]. . . . This reading changed my life. . . . I realized I had never before encountered an architect who not only designed superb spaces, but who was also committed to. . . . one third of the population of the earth. . . . Three years passed before I was to meet Fathy. . . . In late 1975, I wrote to Hassan Fathy in Cairo requesting permission to document his work. . . . He met me at the airport. . . . [and] I set to work reading his voluminous papers, questioning him, and assisting in his work sessions with younger architects.[1]

Hassan Fathy has only one building in the United States, the superb mosque in Abiquiu, New Mexico. It was begun in 1980 and built by Fathy-trained and trusted associates. The commission for a New Mexico project was only partially realized because, at that time, local zoning did not allow for the planned community of houses that were to surround the mosque. Fathy died nine years later at the age of 89. A few months after his death Swan organized a memorial celebration for his life and work at the Cathedral of St. John the Divine in New York City where Charles Moore, Ralph Nader, and Prince Charles took part. At some point

continued on page 41

Hassan Fathy. Dar al Islam. The great Egyptian architect's only building in the United States. Abiquiu, New Mexico. 1981.

[1.] *Aramco World.* "Hassan Fathy's Elegant Solutions." Houston, TX, Vol. 50, #4. July/August 1999.

Courtesy: Adobe Alliance

Courtesy: Adobe Alliance

Top: Camacho House. Ojinaga, Chihuahua, Mexico. Jesusita Jiménez, after being introduced to and taught construction of Nubian vaults and domes by Simone Swan, passed the techniques on to Daniel Camacho Rodríguez and both constructed this model of affordabel housing.

Left: The house of Daniel Camacho Rodríguez, owner and co-builder, who became in the process of construction so enamored of adobe that he is now a sun-dried, adobe brick manufacturer.

Simone Swan. Swan House, 1998. Presidio, Texas.
South elevation and the main entrance from the fire ring and
agave promenade.

Courtesy: Adobe Alliance

Simone Swan. Swan House, 1998. Presidio, Texas.
East elevation with couryard separating the kitchen vault (left)
and the second bedroom vault (right).
Insert. Simone Swan teaching the first step in vault construction
using small adobe bricks. 1994. Ojinaga, Mexico.

Simone Swan. Swan House, 1998. Presidio, Texas.
West elevation and enclosed courtyard separating the master
bedroom vault (left) and the living room vault (right).

Simone Swan. Swan House, 1998. Presidio, Texas.
Top: West courtyard with stairway leading to the roof deck.
Left: West courtyard from the roof deck.

Insert courtesy: Adobe Alliance

Simone Swan. Swan House, 1998. Presidio, Texas.
East elevation vault and mud plaster detail.
Insert: Beginning of vault construction, 1997-1998.

Simone Swan. Swan House, 1998. Presidio, Texas.
View over vault and ocotillo shade screen to the domed guest
house.
Left: Worker constructing one of the parabolic vaults.

Insert courtesy: Adobe Alliance

Simone Swan. Swan House, 1998. Presidio, Texas.
Top: Interior view of one of the dome's squinches and detail of brick work.
Insert: Jesusita Jiménez constructing the guest house dome.
Right: Domed guest house.

Insert courtesy: Adobe Alliance

Simone Swan. Swan House, 1998. Presidio, Texas.
South elevation with the house's main entrance and terrace con-
necting with the domed guest house.
Insert: Livingroom vault during construction.

Simone Swan. Swan House, 1998. Presidio, Texas.
Top and right: Main hall with truss-roof connecting to the
vaulted wings.

Courtesy: Adobe Alliance. Photo: Martine Julien

Simone Swan. Swan House, 1998. Presidio, Texas.
Vaulted livingroom.

Simone Swan. Swan House, 1998. Presidio, Texas.
Roof parapet overlooking a south-facing vault. The adobe lat-
ticework of the parapet allows wind to circulate over the
roof for cooling and ventilation.

Simone Swan. Swan House, 1998. Presidio, Texas.
Top: South elevation courtyard and kitchen vault.
Botton: Windmill mast and solar collectors connected with the
vaulted power shed where batteries and equipment are sheltered.

after the 1990 memorial and before 1994, Swan decided to carry on his work in the border cities of Presidio, Texas and Ojinaga, Chihuahua and founded the Swan Group, a precursor to Adobe Alliance. She has said that during the memorial service she came to question: "Who, I wondered, was carrying out [Fathy's] most vital wish, the very task of helping the poor of this world to be housed decently? No one was doing the work! I resolved then, quite simply, to continue it myself. I was aching to do hands-on building, and to realize materially the learning I had acquired."

The Camacho House

Swan, having fallen in love with the Big Bend region, and having volunteered and gotten her hands muddy in restoring Presidio's historic adobe Fort Leaton, had a fortuitous crossing with Daniel Camacho Rodríguez. At a public housing meeting in Ojinaga, Swan made a presentation showing how traditional adobe with Nubian vaults and domes could be built to perform better (and cheaper) than modern materials in the harsh Chihuahan environment. She presented the idea of affordable and ecological houses—more efficient and much more beautiful than the common cinder block government sponsored houses of the area, or their alternative, mobile homes. After the meeting Camacho came up to Swan and said: "I have some land. I need a house, but I don't have a steady job. If you'll give me the materials, I'll help build the house. Then you'll have a prototype and you can have people visit it whenever you want."

Beginning in April 1995, after Jiménez's

eight months of construction as designed by Swan, Camacho's house was completed—a four-room dwelling with two enclosed courtyards. Using both vaulted and domed space, the interior took on far greater perceptual space than its dimensional size would lead one to think, while additionally taking on the architectural impact of curved, enclosed rooms with their greater air circulation and thermal adobe protection. A win-win situation had materialized: Camacho got a house and the Swan Group got its first case study structure. This structure, Swan calls it Prototype One, was followed by a larger project on the US side of the border that Swan built for herself: Prototype Two.

The Swan House

As it became clear to Swan that the Swan Group should evolve into an educational organization, she created the Adobe Alliance. Her intention was to locate it on the site where she wanted to build her house, 500 acres outside the town of Presidio with the Rio Grande in the distance. After walking the land and learning its environmental strengths and weaknesses—strong winds and blazing heat as well as the breathtaking sunsets and deep isolation—she decided on a construction site and began to consolidate her ideas for the house into the reality of her chosen plot of earth. Unlike many traditional Spanish-influenced, Mexican houses that face into an interior courtyard, the Swan house is configured in an H shape with branches sprouting from a central trunk. In plan, the rectangular, interconnecting spaces articulate different living and working areas, while the central hall not only unites the spaces it serves, but also pumps heart-like vitality into the traffic flows channeled between them. There is drama in this central space that melds the life of the vaulted arm-branches back with the house's high, flat-roofed central hall—a drama made physical by the space's comforting, deep shade when entered from a hot, bright afternoon.

These spaces, considered volumetrically, rise in elevation as arched, earthen chambers, almost like shells or cocoons sheltering the kitchen, living room, master bedroom, and guest room. Geometrically, Swan created a dramatically high, central-hall house with even more extraordinary vaulted spaces. The H footprint creates a building whose arm-branches distribute the overall surface-area, making the 1600 square-foot interior seem much bigger, while the same configuration, considered as distributed exterior surface, reduces solar exposure at the same time that it creates shaded microclimates and wind blocks. Equally dramatic, the exterior walls describe semi-enclosed outdoor garden or patio areas, while the latticed, adobe parapet around the central hall's roof deck opens to let air circulate across and ventilate the roof. So, in real terms, almost every aspect of the building is functioning as a passive environmental device mediating weather even as it graciously encloses living/working space. This house is a kind of organism living on and collaborating with its Texas mesa site.

Even though the plan is not complex it has the effect of creating diverse exterior spaces that, depending on the time of day and the sun's orientation, become more—or less—habitable as outdoor rooms. This makes for differing circulation patterns leading to and from the rooms, hall, patios, and front portal—as one outside space becomes blazingly hot or overwhelming bright, another gradually turns shadier and cooler. The southwest façade portal, or latticed porch, shades the full length of the house from afternoon sun at the same time that it makes for a covered patio oriented to the sunsets and connecting across an agave lined walkway with a large circular fire pit. For more panoramic views and for stargazing, Swan built an exterior stairway between the vaulted master bedroom and the living room that leads to the roof deck atop the central hall. Below that deck, the house's doors open to the north, east, south and west making exterior spaces and the site's system of trails part of a network of circulation routes that in turn multiply the spatial and circulatory presence of the building.

It's important to note that Prototype Two is a passive solar building—no air conditioning—in a landscape where summer temperatures routinely reach 105+ degrees and 130 degrees is not unknown. When taking heat into consideration, the passive-mechanical functioning of the vaults and their thermal adobe properties become critical for the livability of the house. Their height, interior shade, and airflow take on deeper design significance than solely the drama of their architectural shape and height. These are not just pretty forms. Having evolved through centuries of Egyptian design trial and error, the vaults are fit survivors for Presidio's heat. Yet the designs Swan learned from Hassan Fathy, even though they evolved in a similarly hot geography, had not previously been imported into domestic architecture in the United States; and, in fact, before Fathy's difficult search for master masons to build them at the start of his practice in the early 1940s, they had been nearly lost in Egypt.

What we experience in the Swan house is not only the exhilaration of 14.5 foot high curving ceilings but also the constructive logic of Egyptian desert architecture compatible with traditional American adobe building and, ultimately, with American life styles. Swan, thus has recognized a beautiful, foreign architectural form that also makes environmental sense for some domestic building, and she has created demonstration models. The Swan House can be looked at as a case study house in terms of re-imaging Southwestern architecture in an ecological frame as well as with a new emphatic green aesthetic. For her, Prototype Two is an educational working model; for me it is the Swan House, a document of resolution and thinking of one woman determined to follow principles she believes in. And, as such, the Swan House is in the category of Taliesin West and Arcosanti—albeit on a much more modest scale—as an expression of principles and intelligence attached to the goal of teaching. So total is Swan's transference, understanding, and application of Fathy's principles that her Nubian vault architecture looks appropriate, welcome— almost native—in the environment. (The same goes for the adobe domes Swan builds that I'll come to soon.) In my opinion, the potential of

Swan's adaptive and evolving techniques should lead to the Swan House becoming, like its big brothers, Taliesin and Arcosanti, not merely a pilgrimage destination but a regional center for study. In the case of the Swan House, it functions as a study center for traditional forms and materials. Furthermore it could, with Adobe Alliance's support, function as a research center studying the possibility of adapting adobe to new situations, potentially with newly evolved technologies, that further extend Swan's work deeper into areas of sustainability, permaculture, affordability, and biomimetic design.

Construction of the Swan House began in 1997 and, allowing for experimentation, took 18 months. The important stages after the actual design included: 1) decisions about the adobe bricks and their foundation footing; 2) decisions determining the thickness of the tall central hall and vault-supporting walls; 3) truss design and building to span the central hall; and, most critical for this building, 4) the vault construction, with particular attention to the form and framing infrastructure with specially made, smaller adobe bricks (10 x 7 x 2.5 inches). Finally, 5) a decision about and formula for the earth plaster to finish the exterior—something able to withstand heat, periodic torrential rains, and the occasional violent hailstorm.

Some of the construction photographs shown here illustrate the building process as interesting in itself—especially the illustrations of the tapering Nubian vaults as the adobe bricks are angled side-by-side and gently curved to complete the bending arch (not cantilevered as in other vault construction). These vaults create a profile slightly more elongated and slightly more tapered than vaults in Roman or Spanish/Mexican tradition, where profiles are semi-circular. Nubian vaults are designed by hanging a chain between the upper corners of the end wall of the hall that the vault will eventually cover. The hanging chain determines a parabolic arch. The outline of the chain-arch is traced on cardboard and inverted, stood up, so that the downward curve is now an overhead arch. This arch outline is transferred to the back wall where it will serve as a template from which to extend the adobe vault. Recall the *Encyclopedia Britannica*'s definition of a vault as a continuous arch. The parabolic determination of the arch, along with other technicalities of Nubian vault construction, is taught by Swan at specialized workshops, usually conducted yearly or sometimes alternating with dome construction and earth plaster workshops.

Construction of the Swan House was not merely inspired by the goal of a beautiful house—unique as it is—rather, it was guided (and remains so) by an educational process—hands-on experimentation with construction methods and material development as well as the assembling of a team of skilled workers willing in turn, to experiment with new methods of construction and hybridized materials. This process of self-education and educating of others drives Swan in her running of Adobe Alliance. And as the learning curve reflects successes and failures, her building stands to document the process and encourage others to follow its path or a related trajectory. Swan uses the building not only to exhibit success but to point out mistakes. In this sense, as a proselytizing structure for better construction, local environmental concerns, low impact building, beauty, and sustainability, the Swan House has become an icon for Adobe Alliance and the site a research base as well as the destination of increasing numbers of architectural pilgrimages.

Before starting the house, Swan built the little domed adobe structure that now sits almost appended to the house. When I asked her why begin with a 10 x 10 foot structure, she said: "We needed a place to lock up the tools at night." Designing and siting a small domed structure adjacent to the house site, Swan knew she would have an integrated laboratory to illustrate adobe vault, dome, and squinch construction side by side. While both could have been integrated into a single structure, as they were at the earlier Camacho house, the impact of the freestanding, domed-cube building takes on geometric importance far beyond its physical size, especially when seen accompanying the parabolic vaults. This tiny building now serves Swan as a second guest room, but it could equally be a reading room, study, or meditation dome. And it gives animation to the geometries of architecture that Swan can demonstrate and produce as well as giving her site a kind of architectural hot spot—a *punctum* in Roland Barthes's term. While the house vaults are the more articulate structure for covering large, long spaces and surely the most efficient between the two, the little dome provides a romantic shape focus that enters into a geometric conversation with the vaults, benefiting the overall built landscape as a whole. The domed-cube becomes the immediate center of attention while the vaults do the heavy spatial work in the background. Together, like extended mounds of earth, the vaults and dome become a kind of geographic marker in a landscape of creosote bushes and prickly pear cactus, a human burrow, a mud nest in the environment.

Earth Plaster Workshop

While the isolation of a site outside Presidio guarantees that the idle curious will bypass the Swan House, the fact that Marfa, Texas and its cultish art-world reputation—spurred by Donald Judd's permanent sculptural and architectural installations (now open to the public through the Chinati Foundation), its renovated Paisano Hotel and boutique Thunderbird Motel, the wonderful Marfa Book Company, the town's few good restaurants and galleries, as well as Marfa's hosting international literary stars and scholars sequestered in the Lannan Foundation's writers-in-residence program—all only fifty-nine miles from Presidio—ensures that a pilgrimage to Adobe Alliance need not take place in a cultural vacuum. Those who venture to Marfa may or (most likely) may not know about Swan and Adobe Alliance, but those who first venture to Adobe Alliance— probably for one of Swan's regular workshops— surely know or quickly learn about Marfa. And, it is through Marfa as a base that I attended one of Swan's workshops in February 2005.

Top: Marfa, Texas. Middle: Marfa Book Company (cafe & wine bar). Bottom: Donald Judd's Chinati Foundation, Marfa, Texas.

continued on page 64

49

Fire Ring, Swan House. 1998.
Simone Swan (standing center) introduces the agenda for the
February 2005 Adobe Alliance workshop on earth plasters.

Top: Simone Swan (foreground) explains mud plaster ingredients. Jesusita Jiménez mixes plaster ingredients.
Right: Barrels of horse manure tea (top) and macerated prickly pear (bottom).

Construction crew, directed by Jesùsita Jiménez, mixes earth plaster.

Construction crew and workshop participants prepare to apply
first coat of earth plaster to the walls of the domed guest house.

Left and above: Construction crewman demonstrates the techniques for earth plastering. Note the crevice in the dome, just above the wall in this photograph. This crack was caused after extremely wet conditions forced water through a hairline break in the exterior plaster (already removed in the photograph) and water eroded a channel through the adobe. Pointing this damage out to her students, Swan used the crack as an opportunity to discuss adobe repairs and maintenance. The removed plaster contained a small amount of cement which ultimately caused the problem, since cement creates a vapor barrier that holds moisture under its surface. Earth plasters, on the other hand, allow vapor to evaporate and pass back into the environment, thus greatly reducing this type of damage.

Workshop members plastering the adobe dome.

Workshop members plastering the adobe dome.

Construction crew and workshop members plastering the adobe dome.

Adobe Alliance Earth Plaster workshop members.
February 2005.

Since writing this essay, not learning earth plastering, was my initial goal (though after Swan's workshop I can think of little else but mudworks), I based myself in Marfa in order to be able to write about the town as a cultural oasis near Presidio. From Marfa I commuted to the Swan House, but most folks attending Swan's workshops stay closer and many camp out near the house, thus making evening conversations around a group meal and bonfire part of the experience.

Still, the workshop, not Marfa, was my primary motivation for traveling to Texas. I wanted to see how students related to Swan in order to connect my own experiences to observations and then to conversations with her about building and environment and the possibilities of a small organization and a single, determined person's effecting change in a field such as architecture. All this, I soon realized, was beyond the scope of a few days visit—just as documenting which butterfly created the hurricane a continent away in Chaos Theory is. What I did discover was that Swan, Jiménez, and Adobe Alliance were effectively transferring information, techniques, formulas, opinions, and enthusiasm to new and receptive students, and just as the butterfly's wings change air currents, Swan's knowledge reverberates (and will continue to reverberate) in unexpected locations and in unexpected ways. With her educational system in place, Swan's early motivation to go to Cairo, document Hassan Fathy's work and thoughts, and her later determination to use that experience in order to build and teach after his death have been implemented and are still gaining momentum.

The first day of the workshop found some twenty people milling around the Swan House, introducing themselves to each other and chatting. Experience levels varied in this group from no knowledge of adobe to builders with other techniques who came out to see what and how Swan was building. After the introductions and a little exploring around the house and dome, we gathered at the fire pit and Swan introduced herself, Adobe Alliance, and, with the same ease and fluidity she demonstrates when speaking to you privately, she opened the group for each of us to introduce ourselves and for each of us to note specific areas we were interested in. By this time Jiménez and her crew had been working for a couple of hours getting materials ready and beginning to mix plaster, so after a brief tour to points around the house where plasters had failed and where they had succeeded, Swan lead us to the working area and introduced the group to Jiménez.

Opuntia macrocentra. Purple prickly pear on the site of the Swan House; one of the ingredients used in Swan's earth plaster.

From this point the workshop moved very quickly. We were standing by a big pile of sifted clay, a pile of sand, a mound of chopped sorghum (wheat straw is normally used) and two large barrels. One barrel was full of roughly chopped, prickly pear cactus submerged in water. The prickly pear had been harvested by Swan three days before and left to macerate into a slimy liquid. The second barrel was full of a highly diluted liquid of fresh horse-manure "tea." Swan discussed the ingredients, fielding questions as the cement mixer churned the ingredients—water, cactus juice, tea, clay, sand, and sorghum. After being churned for ten or fifteen minutes, the earth plaster was ready to pour into a wheelbarrow and be rolled to the construction site.

Swan uses her successes and mistakes to illustrate building and materials. While two years ago, unhappy with the plaster formula on the vaults and central hall of her house, she decided to strip the original protective, plaster coating (it had contained a small amount of cement, 1/9th I think she said, and had not weathered well). But, at that time, she had not skinned the dome-cube of the same cement-laced plaster and had found major damage in 2004 after an unusually wet year. So, before our arrival she had the plaster chipped off the dome building and left that little structure as our learning laboratory. In re-plastering the house, she had used the formula that had just been recreated for us by Jiménez's crew, and we could look to the house when questions came up about the mud we were applying and its dried properties. For example, the main house looks almost furry with straw showing in the plaster (photo pp. 28-29) so almost all of us wanted to know why straw is part of adobe plaster. We learned that short sections of straw add strength and divert the flow of rainwater over the surface, causing water to continually change directions—thus keeping it from incising a single, deep channel that could penetrate through the plaster and reach the adobe bricks, where structural damage could be severe.

Gathering around the dome, we watched Jiménez and crew demonstrate how to apply the wet mud, how to initially smooth it by hand and then trowel the surface, and later, how to do a second coat and smooth it. While Swan had only intended this novice group to work on the walls, about half the workshop crew got up on scaffolds and began working on the actual dome and squinches. One participant, Richard Hinkel, monkeyed up to the dome's very tip and plastered the most difficult areas. By the end of the second day the dome-cube was plastered and completed—but that's a bit ahead of my chronology.

Friday's last event was a tour of the inside of the Swan House with discussions based on different construction details and techniques. After looking at the interior vaults and the central hall's truss-roof construction, we gathered in the living room for further discussion and questions. Swan began talking about Hassan Fathy and his book *Architecture for the Poor* and some of the possibilities and potential not yet experimented with by Adobe Alliance—for example, a cooling tower to capture prevailing winds, forcing them across a wet surface and directing that passively cooled air into the house. Such cooling towers as well as wind-harvesting towers are common in the Middle East as structural types and well-known and tested in Fathy's work. Furthermore, it seemed to be the group consensus that building a cooling tower would be a good next experiment for Adobe Alliance but one, obviously, for another workshop.

During this discussion, John Morony, a Texas biologist, discussed adobe as a material with properties that in science are known as "phase changes." Morony explained phase changes with the example of water moving through phases of ice, liquid, and vapor, where the constituent mol-

John J. Morony. "Adobe and Latent Heat; A Critical Connection." Unpublished manuscript, revised: November 2004.

ecules remain the same but their molecular order slightly changes density and arrangement. He then went on to discuss adobe as a material that in the mornings, when humidity is generally higher than in the afternoons, absorbs vapor molecules from the air and holds them as a liquid (phase change). In the afternoon as the day heats up, the brick then slowly releases its liquid moisture as a vapor, thus contributing its cooling properties to the building's atmosphere. This phase change accounts for the much more dynamic performance of adobe in cooling when compared to other materials, such as cinder block. (For me, this became a very interesting conversation that placed adobe in a category of advanced materials consistent with my earlier outline in the introduction stressing the need to consider mud as a material ripe for advanced biomimetic experimentation.)

On Saturday we again gathered around the fire pit. The morning would be devoted to final plastering—more hands-on work while that afternoon we would all get a chance to build an adobe wall and corner to fill out the experience of earth building. We learned that the mortar used to build is simpler (only mud and water) than that mixture I described for plastering. Workshop team members got a feel for the bricks, their placement, and how to use bricks that break in two or three sections at the same time as gaining some building experience. By the end of the afternoon, the mid-February morning coolness had changed to warm and sunny, so after cleaning up and making a trip into Presidio for beer and ice cream, the group settled either around the fire pit and a raging bonfire or under the portal and talked and waited while another part of the group cooked up a feast.

It seems that Swan is very open while putting her workshops together; allowing room in her programming to press into duty the attendees she comes to know during their enrollment. In this manner she is able to bring other voices and disciplines to the workshop's discussions. So it was earlier in the day that David Keller, an environmental historian based in Alpine, Texas, was pressed into service and gave an instructive lecture on the geographic history of the Big Bend area we were working in — giving a perspective to geologic time and mineral and volcanic activity that formed the area. And, so it was that, as we relaxed and talked before dinner, a significant discussion sprang up between Morony and Amy Pilling, an expert on permaculture, the former dean of Ecoversity, and one of Swan's inductees for a lecture that had not yet found time to materialize. Informally, and open to the entire, interested group, Pilling outlined some of the tenets of permaculture with citations and examples directed to Morony's site and questions. Most interesting in this respect was her relating building to early site analysis, where both environment and the eventual architecture could be introduced to each other after considering such things as soil remediation and/or conservation, weather patterns, microclimate, native vegetation, prevailing winds, water run-off, waste management, and solar orientation as well as provisions for long-term use of the site around the house; for example: types of gardens and types of eventual land use that will accompany the dwelling. Such a list is only a portion of what Pilling discussed, but what she was careful to outline was that no single area or activity was isolated, that all needed to be considered within the context of the environment. In an earlier private conversation with her, she had already made clear that these principles were not merely active for a single site but needed to be applied at large scales—fused into social systems, cultural traditions, economics, and village and city planning. What Pilling really introduced to the workshop was the seed for a larger view of building that she and Swan see as a way of effecting change compatible with Swan's emphasis on environmental housing, and they see this change being initiated and carried out in small steps that anyone can begin with.

With some of us having to travel home on Sunday the last day was arranged for discussion and later touring of local historic adobe sites, including Fort Leaton, where Swan had begun her Presidio immersion into adobe, design, education, and building politics.

Conclusion

Simone Swan has created much more than I have dealt with above. She has worked to introduce the possibility of including Nubian vaults and/or domes into projects by other architects or contractors, and she (and Jiménez) have a scattering of projects in the West Texas area. She has taken the goals of Adobe Alliance and participated in annual conferences such as those sponsored by The Adobe Association of the Southwest. She has collaborated with institutions such as Ecoversity in

Santa Fe, New Mexico, where in the late summer of 2004 she taught dome building in one portion of a workshop. And Swan inspired María Jesús Jiménez's trip to demonstrate dome building at the Smithsonian Institution in Washington, D.C.

In a sense different from that of an architectural practice, Swan has created a kind of practicing advocacy group for adobe buildings, using principles and forms learned from Hassan Fathy. She has not attempted to mimic a building practice like that of the great architect but to take and understand several of his principal forms and introduce them into a cultural setting where they can interact for the betterment of architectural function and aesthetics. As a new kind of practicing advocacy group, Adobe Alliance is able to support new roles for women in construction; it can take a voice in developing ideas for new environmental actions; it can build demonstration models—a form of practicing what they preach. In a sense, Swan has invented a stealth organization that is poised for collaboration—basing actions, education, material experimentation, and full-scale building in the realm that always echoes: Adobe is Political.

Bibliography

• "Adobe Brick Roofs Introduced to Area." *Alpine Avalanche*. Alpine, TX. January 1, 1998.

• Angelini, Surpik. "Dwelling Inside/Outside the Cultural Body." *Desert Candle*. Alpine, TX. Spring 2005.

• "Building with the People." *Blue Devil Times*. Presidio High School, January 1998, Vol. 1, #3.

• Bonavita, Fred. "From the Earth, Workshop Participants Get a Real Feel Adobe, An Ancient Building Material." *San Antonio Express-News*. San Antonio, TX. March 5, 2005.

• Davidson, John. "Simone Swan Adores Adobe." *Preservation Magazine*. Washington, DC. March/April 1999, #52.

• Davidson, John. "The Promise of Adobe." *Texas Co-Op Power*. Austin, TX. August 1999.

• Davidson, John. "Simone Swan Believes that an Egyptian Architect Would Have Been Right at Home in Arid West Texas." *Texas Co-op Power*. Austin, TX. August 1999: 5.

• "Vaulted Adobe House in Ojinaga Open to Visitors through 1996." *Desert Candle*. Alpine, TX. March 1996.

• Doughty, Dick. "From the Nile to The Rio Grande." *Aramco World*. Houston, TX. July/August 1999: 46.

• Holstrom, David. "Adobe Domes Rising." *Christian Science Monitor*. Boston, MA. March 1, 2000.

• Moore McGregor, Suzi. *Living Homes, Sustainable Architecture and Design*. San Francisco: Chronicle Books. 2001: p70.

• Miller, Lauraine. "Homes from the Earth." *Houston Chronicle Magazine*. Houston, TX. July 12, 1998.

• Mostaedi, Arian. *Sustainable Architecture, Low-tech Houses*. Links International. Barcelona, Spain. 2002.

• Laughlin, Joyanna. "Desert Serenity." *Natural Home*. Loveland, CO. Dec-Jan 2004-2005.

• Novovitch, Barbara. "Bringing Domes to Adobe Homes." *The Japan Times*. Tokyo, Japan. February 28, 2001.

• Szilagi, Pete. "Adobe Abode Built on Vision of Community." *Austin-American Statesman*. Austin, TX. May 17, 1996.

• "Usando técnicas egípicas Simone Swan intenta construir casas se adobe para familias de pocos recursos economicos. La presidencia municipal apoyora la construccion de casa modelo." *Sol de Ojinaga*. Ojinaga, Mexico. 1991.

• Swan, Simone. "A Barrel-Vaulted Adobe Prototype." *Adobe Journal*. Albuquerque, NM. Spring 1997.

• Swan, Simone. "Elegant Solutions." *Aramco World*. Houston, TX. July/August 1999.

• Swan, Simone. "The Merry Pranks of Scholarly Mud Freaks." *Desert Candle*. Alpine, TX. Spring 2005.

• Welch, Frank. "Hands On." *Texas Architect*. Austin, TX. November/December 1998: 38.

• "Egyptian Vernacular Vault Rises in Texas: Hassan Fathy Student Demonstrates Roofing Techniques." US/ICOMOS #7 Newsletter (International Council on Monuments and Sites, US Committee.) Washington, DC. 1992.

• Woodson, Michael. *Living Arts: Interview with Michael Woodson*. Pacifica Radio, KPFT Houston. Houston, TX. March 30, 2005.